Grasslands

THE WORLD'S BIOMES

Deserts

Grasslands

Oceans

Rainforests

Wetlands

THE WORLD'S BIOMES

Grasslands

Kimberly Sidabras

MC **Mason Crest**
Philadelphia

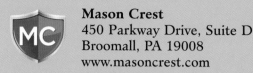

Mason Crest
450 Parkway Drive, Suite D
Broomall, PA 19008
www.masoncrest.com

© 2019 by Mason Crest, an imprint of National Highlights, Inc.

Printed and bound in the United States of America.

CPSIA Compliance Information: Batch #B2018.
For further information, contact Mason Crest at 1-866-MCP-Book.

First printing
1 3 5 7 9 8 6 4 2

Library of Congress Cataloging-in-Publication Data

Names: Sidabras, Kimberly, author.
Title: Grasslands / Kimberly Sidabras.
Description: Philadelphia : Mason Crest Publishers, [2018] | Series: The
  world's biomes | Audience: Age 12. | Audience: Grades 7 to 8. | Includes
  bibliographical references and index.
Identifiers: LCCN 2017047691 (print) | LCCN 2017050707 (ebook) | ISBN
  9781422277522 (ebook) | ISBN 9781422240373 (hardcover)
Subjects: LCSH: Grassland ecology—Juvenile literature.
Classification: LCC QH541.5.P7 (ebook) | LCC QH541.5.P7 S53 2018 (print) |
  DDC 577.4—dc23
LC record available at https://lccn.loc.gov/2017047691

THE WORLD'S BIOMES series ISBN: 978-1-4222-4035-9

QR CODES AND LINKS TO THIRD-PARTY CONTENT

Table of Contents

KEY ICONS TO LOOK FOR:

Words to understand: These words with their easy-to-understand definitions will increase the reader's understanding of the text while building vocabulary skills.

Sidebars: This boxed material within the main text allows readers to build knowledge, gain insights, explore possibilities, and broaden their perspectives by weaving together additional information to provide realistic and holistic perspectives.

Educational Videos: Readers can view videos by scanning our QR codes, providing them with additional educational content to supplement the text. Examples include news coverage, moments in history, speeches, iconic sports moments and much more!

Text-dependent questions: These questions send the reader back to the text for more careful attention to the evidence presented there.

Research projects: Readers are pointed toward areas of further inquiry connected to each chapter. Suggestions are provided for projects that encourage deeper research and analysis.

Series glossary of key terms: This back-of-the-book glossary contains terminology used throughout this series. Words found here increase the reader's ability to read and comprehend higher-level books and articles in this field.

 Words to Understand

aerate—to break up the soil so that air can get in.

apical shoot—a shoot at the tip of a plant.

carnivorous—a carnivorous animal eats other animals for food.

classified—when living things are sorted into groups and given names, based on their relationships.

grazing—eating grass.

herbivores—animals that eat plants.

larva (plural larvae)—the first stage in the life of an insect, after hatching from the egg.

mollusk—any of a group of animals that are soft-bodied and often have shells. They include slugs, snails, clams, mussels, squids and octopuses.

predator—an animal that hunts and kills other animals.

1

A buffalo herd grazes on prairie grass in the Maxwell Wildlife Refuge near Canton, Kansas. All over the world, grasslands have been taken over by people, to grow food or raise farm animals.

What Are Grasslands?

G rasslands are the most widespread biome on land, covering one-fifth of the land surface. They are areas where grasses are the dominant plants. There are relatively few species of grasses, but each grows in huge numbers, densely packed together. Directly or indirectly, grasses provide a very large proportion of human food.

Grasslands first appeared about 65 million years ago, during the Cenozoic era. This was a time when the Earth's climate was becoming cooler and drier. Grasslands cover land that is too dry to support trees, which need a damp climate, but is not so dry as to be desert. The main types of grassland are temperate and tropical grasslands. Temperate grasslands include the prairies of North America, the pampas of Argentina and the cool steppes of eastern Europe and Asia. Tropical grasslands range from the Sahel, where sparse clumps of grass struggle to survive among stunted bushes on sandy ground, to the vast

Australian outback and the East African savannah, an open grassy plain dotted with trees.

How Grasslands Survive

Even in an ideal climate, grasslands cannot survive without regular disturbance. The most common is fire, started by lightning during a dry period. Unless grasslands are periodically burned, shrubs and trees invade them. If the trees are far enough apart the area is savannah, a form of grassland, but when the trees grow closely the grass cannot get enough sunlight to grow, and woodland takes over. Fire kills off tree saplings, but grass quickly recovers from burning.

The other factor that keeps grasslands open is *grazing*. Herds of millions of wildebeest in Africa eat and trample tree seedlings before they can grow. (In the past, herds of bison did the same job on the North American prairies.) The grazers eat the grasses, but this does not kill the grass plants.

Some grasslands were created and maintained by people from prehistoric times. The North American prairies were kept open by Native American hunters. Observing that animals came to feed on the fresh shoots after a natural fire, they realized that they could attract animals to hunt by starting fires themselves. Other grasslands are maintained as pastures by people grazing livestock. They are *classified* as man-made or semi-natural, as opposed to wild or natural grasslands.

Why Grasslands are Fertile

Grasses grow in places with moderate rainfall, so the nutrients in the soil are not washed away by heavy rain. They build up deep, rich topsoil, and their roots hold the soil in place: even after a flood, the nutrients remain. Natural grasslands feed huge herds of grazing animals, and their droppings fertilize the grass. But trying to feed too many animals, or grow too much food on grasslands can cause serious damage.

In contrast to the loose leaf-litter on the floor of a forest, grassland soil is trodden down by the hooves of grazing animals

 ## Wildfires and Grasslands

Wild fires are spectacular and often frightening events. In forests they can be very dangerous, threatening human homes and lives as well as the animals that live in the forest, and often causing serious damage. Forest fires are difficult to control, because the dense fuel generates a lot of heat.

Grass fires are different: the light fuel burns fast and is soon gone, so that the fire is short and relatively cool. The blackened, smoking ground after the fire looks like a disaster, but many of the animals that live in the grassland can run or fly away and the grass is not seriously harmed. Fresh shoots soon appear, and the cycle of growth can begin all over again.

and interwoven with grass roots. The total length of roots under a square metre of prairie is 24 miles (38 kilometers). Some prairie grasses have deep roots, which are useful in times of drought. These may reach down 10 to 15 feet (3 to 4.5 meters).

Understanding the Ecosystem

The activity in grasslands takes place at three levels—on a tiny scale below the surface, on a larger scale among the grass stems, and on an even larger scale above ground, where grazing animals and their *predators* live. All three levels are rich and complex habitats.

Underground, the dense mat of grass roots is home to vast numbers of burrowing creatures. These include many different

Biome versus Ecosystem

A biome is a very large ecological area, with plants and animals that are adapted to the environmental conditions there. Biomes are usually defined by physical characteristics—such as climate, geology, or vegetation—rather than by the animals that live there. For example, deserts, rainforests, and grasslands are all examples of biomes. Plants and animals within the biome have all evolved special adaptations that make it possible for them to live in that area.

A biome is not quite the same as an ecosystem, although they function in a similar way. An ecosystem is formed by the interaction of living organisms within their environment. Many different ecosystems can be found within a single biome. Components of most ecosystems include water, air, sunlight, soil, plants, microorganisms, insects, and animals. Ecosystems exist on land and in water, with sizes ranging from a small puddle to an enormous swath of desert.

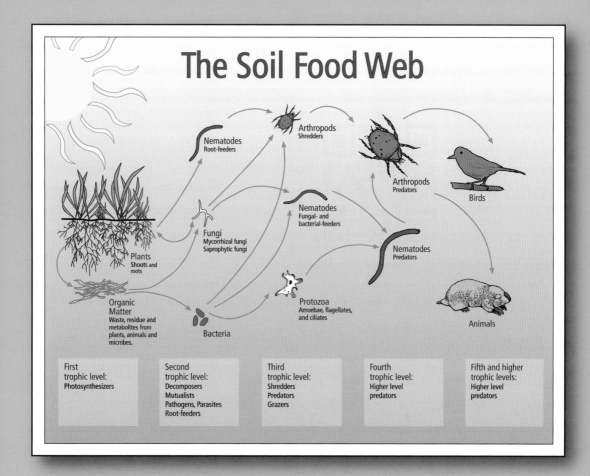

The Soil Food Web

Nematodes
Root-feeders

Arthropods
Shredders

Arthropods
Predators

Birds

Nematodes
Fungal- and
bacterial-feeders

Fungi
Mycorrhizal fungi
Saprophytic fungi

Nematodes
Predators

Plants
Shoots and
roots

Organic
Matter
Waste, residue and
metabolites from
plants, animals and
microbes.

Protozoa
Amoebae, flagellates,
and ciliates

Animals

Bacteria

First
trophic level:
Photosynthesizers

Second
trophic level:
Decomposers
Mutualists
Pathogens, Parasites
Root-feeders

Third
trophic level:
Shredders
Predators
Grazers

Fourth
trophic level:
Higher level
predators

Fifth and higher
trophic levels:
Higher level
predators

species of small roundworms called nematodes. A cubic foot of soil contains about half a million nematodes. Some are predators, but most are *herbivores*, eating the roots of the grass. Nematodes need large amounts of food for their size, and combined with their vast numbers this means that nematodes, not wildebeest or other grazing animals, are the main plant-eaters in grasslands.

In addition to nematodes, grassland soil contains huge numbers of insect *larvae*, mites, and other tiny organisms. They play an important part in maintaining the grassland, by

Educational Video

For an overview of grasslands and the animals that live there, scan here:

breaking down animal and plant wastes into useful nutrients that enrich the soil.

To the animals that live among the stems, grasslands are a forest, a pasture and hunting ground as rich as the tropical rainforests. Mice and voles are the plant-eaters. Weasels and stoats are the top predators, but there are also *carnivorous* beetles and centipedes, hunting insects and small *mollusks*. Just above the ground, birds chase insects and gather seeds.

The large-scale action on the open African savannah is well known, from countless TV wildlife shows. The savannah can be dangerous for prey animals, but it is an easy place to make exciting films. Predators hunt there, and huge herds of grazers wander in search of water and fresh grazing. Crocodiles lurk in the rivers, snatching the migrants as they pass. The herds of wildebeest can be a million strong.

It is difficult to imagine today, but herds as vast as the wildebeest herds in Africa once wandered the North American prairies. At their peak, the prairies were home to 60–70 million bison and 50 million pronghorn antelope. They were preyed on by wolves, bears, mountain lions—and by people.

Why Grasses Are Special

The most important feature of grasses is that unlike most plants they grow from the base, not from an *apical shoot*. When a grazing animal bites off their leaves, grasses continue to grow from a central bud very close to the ground, fuelled by underground food stores. Being cut off near the ground actually stimulates grass to grow, as anyone will know who has a lawn to look after. This enables grasslands to flourish when it is being heavily grazed, or after being burned.

In the tropics, grasses grow during and shortly after the rains, or in some places in the short time when the ground is not flooded. In temperate regions grasses grow best in the spring, between a cool, wet winter and a hot, dry summer. Where the summers are not so hot or dry, as in much of Europe, grasses grow throughout the summer months. As soon as conditions are right, they use their underground energy stores to produce shoots, grow fast, flower and produce seeds. When the seeds have ripened and been dispersed, and if the grass has not been cropped by grazing animals, the top material dies back, leaving the ground covered in a 'thatch' of dead grass. Left alone, this would smother new growth in the following season, and slow down the warming of the ground by spring sunshine in temperate regions. In wild grassland, autumn fires clear away the thatch.

Where Grasslands Are Found

Grasslands can grow in a broad range of climates. Climate also affects the way in which people use grasslands. As well as the temperate prairies and the tropical savannahs, there are some very specialized grasslands dotted round the world.

Typical grassland spreads across rolling or flat country, away from the coast, in areas with moderate rainfall. Tropical

Black-eyed Susan flowers are the tallest "trees" in this miniature forest of prairie plants.

grasslands grow in a climate that has wet and dry seasons, the dry season being the equivalent of the cold winter in colder climates. Temperate grasslands, such as the North American prairies, do not have such a pronounced dry season. In temperate grasslands the diversity of plant species is much less than in the tropics.

In the tropics, trees have evolved that can withstand both grazing pressure and fire, so the grassland here is dotted with trees. This kind of grassland is known as savannah.

The acacia in Africa is a good example of a savannah tree. Its thorny branches have been described as being like a salad made with barbed wire. Few animals can get round the acacia's spiny defenses. Giraffes, with their long, nimble tongues, can pick acacia leaves from between the thorns, while black rhinos have leathery mouths that can crunch up the thorniest twigs. Trees like this are dotted over African grasslands, and tropical grasslands in general.

Paramo Grassland?

In the high Andes of South America, between the subtropical rainforest that reaches to about 5,900 feet (1800 meters) and the snowline above 16,400 feet (5,000 m), there is a temperate zone. The higher parts of this zone, between about 13,100 to 16,400 feet (4,000 to 5000 m), support an area of alpine grassland called the paramo.

At this altitude it is very cold during the day, and freezing every night. The vegetation is short grass dotted with a variety of tiny, often brightly colored flowers. This dramatic scenery,

The acacia tree is adapted to survive on the African savannah.

Sheep and horses graze in the green fields of Patagonia.

where cliffs and gullies divide the rolling grassland, is used by farmers to graze hardy mountain cattle.

The Pampas

Most of eastern Argentina in South America consists of huge flat grassy plains called the pampas. The greater part of the plain, known as the dry pampa, is a salty, sandy wilderness. However, the eastern edge of the pampas, called the humid pampa, is cooler and well-watered. When Spanish settlers arrived in the region, they raised cattle and herds of semi-wild horses on the humid pampa. Gauchos, the famous cowboys of the plains, tended the cattle and horses. Today, the pampa is devoted mainly to growing wheat, maize, and alfalfa. These crops are used to supplement the grazing for herds of pedigree cattle and sheep.

Tussock Grassland

Tussock grasslands grow in New Zealand and on some of the islands just outside the Antarctic Circle, such as South Georgia, Bird Island and the Falklands. A similar form of grassland grows in the tropics, but only on the top of high mountains. Tussock grass, as its name suggests, grows in dense clumps or tussocks, often as much as six feet (two meters) tall. It grows in this way because it has never been grazed by mammals. It is easy to imagine the impact of introducing animals like sheep and deer to previously untouched areas of tussock grassland: large areas have been completely destroyed.

  Text-Dependent Questions

1. How much of the earth's surface do grasslands cover?
2. When did grasslands first appear?
3. What are nematodes? How do they help grasslands?

  Research Project

Select one of the major types of grasslands. Using your school library or the internet, do some research. Where are these grasslands located, and what are some of the characteristics? Write a two-page report that details your findings and present it to your class.

 Words to Understand

annual—a plant that grows, produces seed and dies within a season.

germinate—to grow, like a seed.

herbal—a book that lists many types of plants and their uses.

perennial—a plant that lives on from year to year.

silage—grass that is stored wet and allowed to ferment, and is then used for animal feed.

2

A herd of horses roams the steppe of Mongolia, one of the few places where wild grasslands still exist. Some nomadic Mongolian herdsmen still graze cattle and horses on the grasslands, though many have abandoned their traditional ways and settled in cities.

How Grasslands Are Created

Many grasslands have existed for thousands of years, but this does not mean that they are permanent. To survive, they need constant intervention by outside forces, such as drought, fire or grazing animals. This makes them very suitable for use by humans—and vulnerable to misuse.

In botanical terms, a climax community is one whose members may change as time passes and the environment changes, but which remains essentially the same. Forests and seashores are climax communities, but grasslands are not. If fires no longer happen, for instance, or if grazing animals disappear, grassland will give way to a different type of vegetation.

The process of development of the plant community in an area is called succession. The best way to see succession in action is to clear a plot of land and watch what happens over a period of years. One group of plants flourishes and is succeed-

A wooded area that has been cleared for farming in Madagascar; the trees were cut down and then a controlled fire was set to burn the stumps and vegetation. This process, called "slash and burn," is one of the oldest ways of preparing land for agriculture. By cutting and burning woodland, people produce conditions where grasses will grow—in this case cereals that they will use for food.

ed by another, then another, until eventually a steady state is reached. This is the climax community for that area.

Evolution of a Biome

The first plants to appear on a cleared plot of land are known as "pioneer plants." These are species whose seeds are widely dispersed, perhaps by wind or animals, and *germinate* wherever they land. In a garden, pioneer plants are called weeds.

Nettles, bindweeds, docks, this-tles, and grasses are common pio-neer plants in a temperate climate. They are mostly *annuals*, and they do not survive competition from other plants for long. Left untended, cleared land will quick-ly become mainly grassland, as the grasses overcome and outlive most of the other pioneer plants.

This is not the end of the story. After perhaps three or four years, more competitive plants begin to grow, such as *perennial* herbs and shrubs. They are invaded in their turn by the seedlings of quick-growing trees such as birch and ash. After about fifty years have passed, the cleared plot will have become shady woodland. The suc-cession is still not complete, howev-er, because seedlings of other trees, such as beech and oak, are adapted to grow in these conditions, and they can outgrow and outlive the first arrivals. After another fifty or a hundred years, the area will be a stable forest of beech, oak and ash, the climax community of temperate low-lands. Any change that takes place from now on will be very slow, in a complex ecosystem dominated by long-lived, highly competitive trees.

Foxgloves are "pioneer plants" that flourish in open, sunny places.

When does grassland persist?

For grassland to become established and to persist for any length of time, something has to happen to stop it turning into woodland. We have already seen the way in which fire, drought, or grazing can damage or kill many of the plants that compete with the grass, such as trees and shrubs. The grass, on the other hand, can usually survive these things.

Not all the plants that compete with grasses are wiped out by drought, fires, and grazing. Many species of wildflower survive successfully in grasslands. In fact, three-quarters of grassland plant species are not grasses. Orchids, daisies, buttercups, campions, and knapweeds are just some of the many kinds of wildflower found on temperate grasslands around the world. Orchids are also found in tropical grasslands.

 Educational Video

Scan here for a video on plants that are native to the American prairie:

Plant Survival Mechanisms

Plants that survive in grasslands must have a way of overcoming the threats to their existence. Fire and drought, both of which wipe out tree seedlings, have less effect on plants that have deep storage roots. Thistles are a good example of such plants. They have long, fleshy roots from which they can regrow after being burned away by fire, or shrivelled by drought. Docks and nettles have the same type of storage roots. Nettle roots wander long distances under the ground, and can push up new shoots far from the parent plant.

If such plants are eaten by grazers (or if their tops are cut off by a lawnmower) they quickly grow new leaves. The new leaves produce more food to pack into the plant's storage roots, ready for the next time the plant is damaged.

Thistles have other defenses against grazing animals. They are covered with fine spines, which are painful to sensitive lips. Furthermore, they can grow flat against the ground, so that fires—and lawnmowers—pass over them and leave them undamaged.

Dandelions and daisies are among the first flowers to appear in pastureland. They grow in the spring while the grass is still short.

A large field of poppies and other summer flowers growing in a meadow near Cerne Abbas in Dorset, England. Tall grass is the preferred habitat for poppies. They are beautiful, but most farmers consider them to be weeds.

Other grassland survivors avoid being eaten by having a foul taste. Some of them are actually poisonous to grazing animals. Ragworts and hemlock, for example, are poisonous to many grazing animals.

Other plants are not protected by spines, and their leaves and flowers taste good to grazing animals. Plants like this survive by growing quickly, with their leaves flat against the ground, until they have flowered and produced seeds. The many members of the daisy and dandelion family grow like this, and are very successful survivors in grazed grassland.

Some plants can only survive in grassland that is grazed: if the grass is allowed to grow tall they will not receive enough light, and die out. Many low-growing daisies are like this, as are a number of rare and decorative plants such as orchids. Other plants can only survive if the grasses grow tall. Some types of tall daisies such as marguerites, and vetches and red poppies are plants that like tall grass. Tall-growing plants like these are common weeds of grain crops. However, when grass is cut for hay or for *silage*, such "weeds" are a welcome addition. Hay is mature grass that has been cut and dried; it is stored as feed for cattle. Silage is made by cutting grass and fermenting it to produce valuable winter feed.

Grass Defenses

The deep root system of prairie grass protects it against damage from fire or drought. However, other types of grasses have a dense, tangled mat of shallow roots. They are able to survive grassland fires because these fires do not usually overheat any more than the top few centimeters of soil. Thus even grasses with shallow roots can survive a fire. A tangled mat of roots is also useful in surviving a drought, because the matted roots will hold enough water to keep the grass alive until the rains return.

Grasses have no defense against being grazed. They actually grow best when they are regularly cut or nibbled close to the ground. Grasses are proof against all the forces that hold back the competition. As long as those forces keep up the pressure, grasslands can survive in their incomplete stage of succession. This is what has made grasslands, in all their various forms, the most widespread biome on Earth.

The Value of Wild Grasslands

Humans have taken over most of the world's grasslands, but there are still a few wild areas that have not been affected by human activity. A few other areas, some very small, are being restored to their original condition. Although they are less dramatic than the rainforests, grasslands are just as valuable as other natural biomes.

Grassland soil is naturally very fertile, as the earliest farmers learned when they first grew crops and grazed cattle. They did not understand why the soil was so fertile, or how the fertility could be maintained. We now understand these things a little better, thanks to the study of wild grasslands.

In the Australian outback, most of the grassland has been taken over by huge sheep and cattle stations. The farmed livestock eat all the grass, leaving little for kangaroos, wallabies, and other wild inhabitants.

The complex ecosystems of grasslands and their wide range of plants and animals have a lot to teach botanists and zoologists. Some grassland plants have medicinal value. The plains-dwelling Native Americans used coneflower root as a painkiller and an antibiotic, in fact as a treatment for everything from snakebite to the common cold. It has been found to protect against viruses like influenza, as well as stimulating the immune system. Coneflower is also an effective natural insecticide. European grasslands produce many medicinal plants, and these have been catalogued in *herbals* for hundreds of years.

Where Wild Grasslands Survive

The few remaining natural grasslands of the world have survived because they are too remote and inhospitable for people to have exploited them. Tussock grass on sub-Antarctic islands, for example, is beyond the reach of farmers, and the

  Grassland Gardeners

Earthworms swallow large quantities of soil, to extract bacteria and other single-celled organisms for food. They then pass the soil out of their bodies at the surface as worm casts. This process turns over the soil and *aerates* it. It is amazing that on the North American prairie, the earthworms weigh more than the bison did at their peak. In pastureland in Europe, there is a greater weight of worms per acre than of cattle and sheep.

Another important group of soil-turners, moving as much soil as the earthworms, are harvester ants. These ants build large underground colonies, excavating the soil grain by grain.

paramo is too high up to be over-exploited. Where humans can reach tussock grass, as in New Zealand, it is quickly destroyed, beyond the hope of being restored.

Wild grasslands survive only in sparsely populated areas like the Mongolian plains and the steppes of north-eastern Asia. Even there, they are occupied not by the original grazing animals but by the herds of domestic animals owned by nomadic herders. Large predators are everywhere under pressure, but in other ways these wild grasslands are much as they were before humans intervened.

In Africa, apart from the Sahel, wild grasslands are found in the belt of savannah that forms the setting for many TV features and safari holidays. This is what has saved the area from being farmed: the money it can raise from tourism makes it more valuable as a nature reserve than as farmland.

Grasslands in Europe

There is no truly wild grassland left in Europe, because of human activities. The lowlands have been farmed for thousands of years. Alpine meadows, which are found on steep mountainsides across Europe, are not natural grasslands at all, but semi-natural pastures cleared from the forest hundreds of years ago. Celebrated grassland areas in Britain, such as the South Downs and Salisbury Plain, are also classified as "semi-natural." They were created in the sixth century, when Saxon invaders cut down the forests, and have been maintained since by grazing. Before this time, most of Britain was covered by forest.

This artificial landscape is very beautiful, and with good management a healthy wild flora and fauna can survive alongside intensive human agriculture. If grazing stopped for any reason—perhaps because it became uneconomic on the world market—the whole area would quickly revert to the shrubby woodland of pre-Saxon times, unless it were carefully managed to preserve the grassland.

In a wild grassland, thistles have to grow tall in order to flower and produce seeds. Where the grass is grazed or mowed, thistles have to grow flat against the ground to survive.

In all but a few areas of the North American prairies the grasslands are a human domain. The grasses have been plowed up and turned into farmland. Farmers use machines to plant, grow and harvest wheat, corn, and other crops.

Wild Prairie in America

When Europeans arrived in North America, the prairies covered a quarter of the lower 48 states, and a large part of southern Canada. By the start of the twentieth century, farms could be found on most of the continent, and only small fragments of prairie remained. Illinois, the Prairie State, once contained 37 million acres of virgin prairie; there are now just 3,500 acres (one ten-thousandth) left.

In other states, where the prairie has not been plowed it has become forested. This is because of modern firefighting practices and techniques, which prevent fires from sweeping across the grasslands unchecked. If Americans had followed the practice of the Native Americans, they would have let the prairies burn when lightning set it on fire, or burned the grasslands themselves, to keep down the trees and encourage the growth of new grass.

The South American humid pampas are now all either pastureland or under cultivation. The dry pampas survive in their wild state because these areas are mostly unusable by farmers, though new irrigation techniques threaten even this arid, unproductive land.

Text-Dependent Questions

1. What is a climax community?
2. What are some survival mechanisms that protect grassland plants?
3. How do earthworms and harvester ants help grasslands to thrive?

Research Project

Do some research on grassland plants, using your school library or the internet. What are some ways that these plants have adapted to survive? How do they spread their seeds, or protect themselves from being eaten? Write a two-page report and share your findings with the class.

 Words to Understand

bacteria—microscopic living things that are neither plants nor animals.

chitin—the hard substance that covers insect bodies.

enamel—the hard substance that forms the outer layer of teeth.

fermentation—the breaking down of food by the action of bacteria or yeasts (microscopic fungi).

migrate—to travel regularly to find more suitable conditions.

ruminant—an animal that re-chews its food ("chews the cud"), such as a cow or a deer.

rumination—re-chewing food that has been swallowed once already.

How Animals Live in Grasslands

Grazing animals large and small find an easy living on grasslands. They are surrounded by food as far as the eye can see. They are also surrounded by predators—from lions and pumas that hunt antelope and deer to jackals and coyotes that feed on mice and other small rodents. The key link in this long and complex food chain is the grass that, directly or indirectly, feeds them all.

When grasslands developed in the Cenozoic era, many animals evolved to exploit the new biome. Horses, which had until then been small woodland animals, became large, swift runners. Antelope evolved into many different grass-eaters, some more specialized than others. Much later, a group of woodland primates emerged on to the plains to become savannah hunters and food-gatherers. They eventually evolved into the genus Homo—the original human beings.

Grazing Animals

There is an enormous range of animals that live by grazing, from nimble deer and antelope to ponderous white rhinoceroses and elephants. Horses, too, are highly adapted as grazing animals. Most rely on being able to see long distances and run fast to evade their predators (rhinos and elephants are exceptions), but above all they must be able to eat and digest grass.

Grass stems contain silicon, a tough mineral that wears away teeth. So grazing animals have flat grinding teeth with hard ridges of *enamel* that are very hard-wearing. Many have a way of replacing these teeth when they do eventually wear out.

The cell walls of plants, including grass, are made of a tough substance called cellulose. No mammal can digest cellulose directly. To extract energy from plant food, they need help from *bacteria*, which break down the cellulose for them. This process, called *fermentation*, works in one of two ways.

Most large grazing animals deal with grass by *rumination*. They have a stomach divided into four chambers. They grind up the grass and swallow it into the first chamber (the rumen), where fermentation softens the grass blades. A little later, they regurgitate their food and grind it again, a process known as "chewing the cud." When they next swallow it, it is fine enough to pass through the sieve-like second chamber and into the third and fourth chambers, where it is fermented further. The bacteria take some energy for themselves, but there is plenty left over for the owner of the stomach.

Rumination is very efficient, but it is a slow process. Antelope, deer, cattle, sheep, goats, camels, and giraffes are all *ruminants*. Horses, rhinos, and tapirs use a different process,

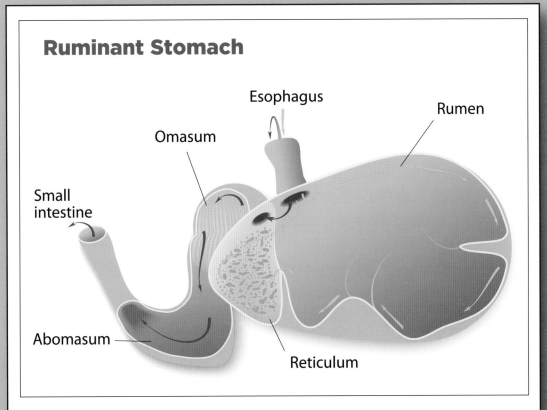

Ruminant Stomach

Esophagus

Rumen

Omasum

Small
intestine

Abomasum

Reticulum

The ruminant species have one stomach that is divided into four compartments: rumen, reticulum, omasum, and abomasum. Ruminating mammals include cattle, goats, sheep, camels, and antelope.

called cecal digestion. Their fermentation chamber is a large bag called the cecum, between the small and large intestines. They pack it with grass, and wait for the bacteria to break it down. However, they do not wait very long: food passes through a horse in 48 hours, whereas it takes 70 to 90 hours in a cow. Cecal digestion is not as efficient as rumination—a horse extracts only 70 percent as much energy from its food as a cow. But by processing larger amounts of food more quickly, the horse can gather the same total amount of energy.

Predators versus Prey

Grassland predators like lions and cheetahs don't eat grass, but they are just as dependent on it for their food as grazing animals. They let the grazing animals digest the grass, and then eat the grazers. Humans also rely on grass indirectly: they use cattle and sheep to change grass into meat and milk.

Wild prey animals have evolved a series of defensive measures to help avoid predators, based mainly on being very alert. Grassland prey animals have good hearing, a keen sense of smell, and a wide field of vision. They are very quick off the mark when danger threatens, and many species can outrun a predator over long distances. Domestic animals, by contrast, have been bred to be calm and to trust people. Some grassland animals avoid predators by living underground. Badgers spend the daylight hours in large burrows called setts. Moles hunt earthworms in the soil, and very rarely come to the surface at

When grasslands emerged, horses were transformed from small, shy woodland creatures into swift runners of the open plains. These wild mustangs live in Montana.

all. Rabbits, gophers and prairie dogs live in huge, complex underground burrow systems, usually emerging to feed at dusk and during the night. The African and European equivalents of prairie dogs are mongooses and marmots. Marmots are rodents, related to squirrels.

The Importance of Rodents and Insects

Rodents are an important group of grassland mammals, partly because they serve as prey for smaller carnivores such as hawks, eagles, coyotes, jackals and foxes. Rodents feed mainly on seeds, but many of them also hunt insects among the grass stems. They serve as a link between the grass at the base of the food chain and predators that are not big enough to catch large grazing animals such as antelope.

Prairie Dogs

In the past, the prairie dogs of North America played a vital part in maintaining the pasture for the vast herds of bison that roamed the region. Prairie dog burrows and droppings aerated and fertilized the land, so that the grass that grew around their burrows (or "towns") was of a higher quality. Bison preferred to graze near prairie dog towns. However, as farmed cattle replaced wild bison, ranchers began to poison prairie dogs because they believed they competed for the grass, when in fact the higher-quality grasses growing around their towns more than made up for what they ate.

At one time, the population of prairie dogs on the prairies of the United States and Canada may have been as high as 1 billion. Today, the prairie dog population is estimated at about 10 to 20 million—a decline of more than 98 percent. In addition to poisonings, the steady reduction of the wild grassland areas of North America has also contributed to the decline of the prairie dog population.

A weasel catches a meadow mouse that had been forced by hunger to leave the safety of its burrow.

Insects are the most successful and varied group of animals in grasslands. Butterflies are very numerous; they feed and breed on wildflowers, not grasses. Grasshoppers and crickets are members of an enormous family, with 17,000 known species, most of them tropical or subtropical. Their bodies are heavily armored against predators with a tough material called *chitin*. They also have long, powerful hind legs for leaping to safety, and if all else fails they can fly away.

Another very successful group of grassland insects feeds on other animals rather than on plants. They are the blood-sucking flies. Some, like botflies, have a complex life cycle. Their eggs are swallowed by grazing animals and develop inside their guts, often causing great distress and sometimes death. Others simply land on their victims and suck their blood. Horseflies are highly adapted to this way of feeding. They fly silently, and land very softly, so that the first their victim knows of their arrival is the sharp pain of the bite—by which time the damage is done.

A vital group of insects where so many large mammals eat grass is the dung beetles. Without them, grasslands would be

Locusts, members of the grasshopper family, are very successful plant-eaters in grasslands. Much of the time they are dull colored and live and feed alone. But some are brightly colored, like this one from the grasslands of South Africa. On the African mainland locusts form huge swarms, which can seriously damage food crops.

The activities of earthworms and insects like the dung beetle help grasslands to thrive.

buried in a layer of droppings so deep that nothing could grow. The adults eat some of the dung, but their larvae account for most of it. Some parent beetles simply lay their eggs in dung piles, while others dig a burrow to bury dung for their larvae to eat when they hatch. Some make large balls of dung, which they roll to the burrow: others simply collect it in mouthfuls. Dung beetles have many predators, including storks and ibises, which probe dung piles in search of the large, luscious larvae.

Grassland Birds

Grassland birds are mostly seed-eaters, and they often use grass blades to weave their nests. The most successful of all is the red-billed quelea, a small finch that lives in Africa. It moves in enormous flocks, often more than a million strong, *migrating* across country to follow the rains. It is the most numerous species of bird on earth: the population is estimated at 1.5 billion. Although each bird weighs less than an ounce (20 grams), and eats only 0.08 ounces (2.5 g) of seeds a day, a large flock can strip the seeds from an area of grass or crops in a very short time. Their colonies of woven grass nests are so huge that they sometimes break the branches of savannah trees.

Grassland plains are also the home to several species of large flightless birds such as ostriches, rheas, emus, bustards, and cassowaries. Wild

Educational Video

For a video on the challenge that grassland birds face, scan here:

A secretary bird hunts a venomous green mamba in South Africa. The bird's long legs, covered in thick, shiny scales, protect it from the snake's fangs.

ostriches are now found only in Africa. They used to live in Syria and Arabia as well, but the last one outside Africa was killed in 1941.

Rheas, which live in South American grasslands, differ from ostriches in having three toes instead of two. The rhea population has fallen considerably in recent years. Rheas and their eggs are often eaten by local people, and they are killed to be used as dog food. Rheas near agricultural areas are also killed, because they will eat almost any crop.

Emus in Australia also have three toes—they still survive in spite of fierce persecution during the early twentieth century, when many emus were killed with machine guns to protect growing wheat.

The Secretary bird, which lives on the African savannah, is not flightless but spends most of its time on the ground. It hunts snakes on foot, stamping them to death with long, armored legs. Other birds of prey search the sea of grass from the air, looking for small mammals or reptiles such as lizards and snakes.

Some birds of prey prefer to eat carrion, or dead animals. African vultures soar over the grasslands watching for carrion. In the southern United States and Central America, huge condors are the American equivalent of vultures.

Text-Dependent Questions

1. What are some differences between rumination and cecal digestion?
2. Why are predators like lions and cheetahs dependent on grasses?
3. How many species of grasshoppers and crickets are there?
4. What is the most numerous grassland bird?

Research Project

In North America, prairie dogs play an important role in keeping grasslands healthy. Using the internet or your school library, find out more about recent efforts to protect prairie dog populations. Write a two-page report on your findings, and share it with your class.

 Words to Understand

feedlot—an area or building where livestock are fed and fattened up.

hybrid—a combination, sometimes called a cross, between two different plants or
 animals.

yurt—a type of tent made of felt or skins, used by nomadic peoples in Mongolia
 and central Asia.

Many grasslands in the United States have been converted to farms, where crops such as corn and wheat can be grown to feed people and animals.

How Humans Use Grasslands

W hen early humans first wandered on the grassy plains, they were hunter-gatherers, finding food where they could. It would be more than a million years before they hit on the idea of planting crops or rearing domestic animals. At some point humans learned that edible seeds and grains could be cultivated in a particular place, so they no longer had to forage far and wide looking for those plants. In this way they discovered a source of food that has been the basis of mankind's diet ever since.

Today, most human populations grow their food on relatively well-watered grasslands that they have adapted for their own use. All cereals are modified grasses. They are bred over many generations to produce larger seeds, which remain on the plant after ripening rather than being shed as they are by wild grasses. Drier grasslands have been used for thousands of years to raise domestic cattle.

The Origins of Farming

Humans began farming in the Middle East about ten thousand years ago, in an area now known as the Fertile Crescent, a hilly, grassy region that curves round the northern edge of the Arabian Desert. A group of hunter-gatherers may have realized that plants grow from seeds, and, in a daring experiment, buried some of their hard-earned collection of wild barley. Or perhaps they were saving the barley to eat later, and returned to find that it had sprouted.

Independently, people planted rice in Asia, and maize (corn) and squashes in America. However they began, these first farmers changed the course of human history. When they no longer had to roam in search of seeds to eat, they could settle in villages. They could tame the wild sheep and goats on the surrounding hills, so that they no longer had to go hunting. Farming had begun.

When people began growing crops and rearing livestock, they found that they had enemies all around. Inedible plants threatened to choke their crops, and bugs and birds ate them. Predators came to steal their sheep and goats. The farmers rooted out the weeds, and did what they could to discourage the pests and drive away or kill the predators.

When they had filled all the available grassland with their crops and pastures, early farmers made more space by clearing woodlands, digging irrigation ditches, and carving terraces (stepped fields) into hillsides. They left their mark on the face of the Earth.

In some places where hillsides were terraced, today's farmers still grow crops on the ancient terraces, which have been in

These rice terraces in northwestern Vietnam may have been cut into the hillside more than a thousand years ago. Small channels allow water to trickle from each terrace to the one below. However, in dry weather water must be carried by hand to the topmost terraces.

place for hundreds, if not thousands, of years.

The Effect of Farmers

The arrival of Europeans immigrants on the plains of North America during the nineteenth century represents the most extreme example of the impact of modern farming methods on grasslands. These immigrants to America were already established farmers, and with the help of the U.S. government they displaced the Native Americans of the Great Plains, who were

Educational Video

To learn about the ancient origins of farming, scan here:

mainly hunter-gatherers. As they did so they transformed the landscape.

Native Americans cultivated crops on a small scale on family plots, but the newcomers grew crops for sale, not just to feed their families. Where the natives had tilled the soil with sharpened sticks, the newcomers used horse-drawn plows. Parts of the prairie were too tough even for these plows, until John Deere invented the steel plow in 1837 and exposed the wonderfully fertile soil beneath the dense prairie surface.

Where their ancestors plucked out weeds and squashed bugs by hand, leaving many survivors, modern farmers spray herbicides and pesticides over huge areas. This can wipe out huge numbers of insects and other creatures, including harmless or beneficial ones. Humans today can produce cereals and meat in quantities far greater than the old farmers could ever have imagined.

Popular Cereal Crops

All cereal crops are *hybrid* grasses (mixtures of more than one type). Wheat, oats and barley are the main cereals in temperate regions, while in warmer countries maize and sorghum are more important. Rice is the most important cereal in terms of the amount produced, but wheat is more important in terms of world trade.

Sorghum is a grass that grows to more than 10 feet (3 meters) in height. It is the staple cereal in large areas of China, India, and Africa, but the world's largest producer is the United States, where it is grown to feed cattle.

Not all crops grown on grasslands are modified grasses. Fields of soybeans or tobacco, and plantations of citrus fruits or pineapples cover millions of acres that were once open grasslands, with all their variety of plant and animal life.

Farmed Grazing Animals

Grasslands around the world support 3 billion domestic animals that are farmed for their meat and/or milk. The most common are cattle, sheep, goats, and camels.

Cattle are raised in enormous numbers because of the worldwide demand for beef. Most meat from farmed cattle is

Cattle hold a special place in some cultures. In some African countries, as well as in Madagascar, cattle are used instead of money, or simply kept as a measure of wealth. An African family that owns a herd of cattle is highly regarded by their neighbors, even though the animals might be close to starving.

used to make hamburgers; the rest goes to supermarkets and restaurants in wealthy countries. Raising beef cattle requires large amounts of grass. In the United States, cattle are often allowed to graze on grass until they reach about 750 pounds (340 kg). After that they are moved onto feedlots, where they live in small pens and eat grain (such as corn) that is brought to them. Once the cattle reach a weight of about 1,300 pounds (590 kg) they are sent to be slaughtered.

Modern veterinary medicine is used to make cattle herds more productive. Antibiotics are given to cattle to keep them healthy even in very crowded conditions. Some cattle are given hormones to make them grow bigger and more quickly. Beef cattle are also bred to grow larger.

Overgrazing

Raising domestic cattle on enclosed areas of grassland is a relatively new development in agriculture. It can cause damage to the pasture known as "overgrazing," in which the grass is grazed and the ground trampled beyond recovery. Wild grazing animals, or domestic herds that are allowed to range widely over large areas, do not cause such harm to grasslands.

The way animals are grazed in Mongolia is a good example of how overgrazing can be avoided. Mongolia is a country of grasslands, where huge plains cover four-fifths of the country. The plains are the home of a wandering nomadic people. They raise herds of sheep, goats and cattle, which they tend on horseback. When the animals have eaten the grazing in a particular area, the herders move them to new pastures.

Mongolian herders set up a village of *yurts*, then graze their animals in groups according to species (sheep, horses, and cattle are taken out separately). The animals graze through the day, working in a spiral out from the village, and are brought back at night. When the journey to the pasture becomes too long for convenience, the whole village packs up and moves to a new location. This protects the grasslands from overgrazing. For many centuries the nomads' animals have provided them with dairy products, meat, wool, and leather.

However, this traditional practice might be coming to an end. The Chinese and Mongolian governments have tried to persuade nomadic herders to settle on farms and ranches, where they can be provided with schools, hospitals, and other modern conveniences. Some nomads are reluctant to leave their traditional lifestyles—they would prefer to maintain their wandering way of life. However, climate changes in

Goats and Overgrazing

Not all farmed animals need grass to survive. Goats can flourish by browsing; eating leaves and twigs from trees and shrubs, rather than eating grass. In areas where overgrazing has degraded the land, goats may be the only livestock that can find anything to eat. However, allowing goats to live on overgrazed land causes serious environmental damage. The goats will eventually destroy the trees and shrubs. In time these overgrazed areas tend to become deserts where very little plant life can grow. This has occurred in various places in Africa, the Middle East, and Asia.

A herd of horses grazes on the rolling grassland of Mongolia. Traditional tent-like dwellings, known as yurts, can be seen in the background.

Mongolia over the past fifty years have resulted in hotter, dryer summers and colder winters, and these changing weather patterns have made it harder for nomads to survive. In 2010, for example, nearly 9,000 Mongolian families saw their entire herds freeze or starve to death during a severe winter, while another 30,000 families lost at least half of their livestock.

In addition, the expansion of urban areas in Mongolia has eliminated some of the traditional grazing lands. For these reasons, between 2005 and 2018 approximately 600,000 Mongolian nomads moved into cities.

A burrowing owl stands near its burrow. Ground-nesting grassland birds like this are in danger from human farming activity.

The Proper Use for Grasslands

Some people argue that growing modified grasses, such as wheat, barley, or pulses (plants like lentils, beans, and peas), produces more protein per acre than rearing livestock for meat and milk. Also, the other costs associated with producing meat are very high. Producing animal protein uses eight times more food energy than it produces. It is estimated that a steer must eat up to twenty-five pounds of grass to produce a pound of beef. Producing grain-fed beef uses fifty times more water than producing rice.

On the other hand, animal protein contains a mixture of nutrients and vitamins that cannot be obtained from a single type of food plant. Also, many grassland areas are unsuitable for growing arable crops. In these places, livestock farming is the only type of food production that is feasible. Most importantly, people like eating meat, particularly in the wealthier nations of the West.

Text-Dependent Questions

1. Where and when did humans begin farming crops and raising livestock ?
2. What are the main cereal crops in temperate regions? What are the main cereal crops in warmer regions?
3. How does overgrazing by cattle and other domestic animals affect grasslands?

Research Project

Some human crops grown from grasses include wheat, rye, oats, rice, corn, and sorghum. Choose one of these grassland cereals and find out more about it, using your school library or the internet. Where is that cereal crop grown, and what methods are used for cultivation? Does the farming of this crop damage grasslands or help them. Write a two-page report with your findings, and share it with your class.

 Words to Understand

erosion—wearing away, either of teeth or of soil and rocks.

scythe—a tool used for cutting crops such as grass or wheat, with a long curved blade at the end of a long pole attached to which are one or two short handles.

Dairy cows graze on an alpine meadow high in the Swiss alps.

Preserving Grasslands

With very few exceptions the remaining natural grasslands of the world survive only because people do not need them. For the time being they are safe, though they could be threatened in the future. The grasslands that need protection today are the semi-natural grasslands, where pressure from farming is increasing.

One of the areas worst affected by overgrazing is the Sahel, a band of grassland across Africa just south of the Sahara Desert. The Sahel has been under heavy grazing pressure for thousands of years. The grasses that made it prime pastureland in ancient times have become rare plants: they now survive only as tiny clumps in rocky areas that livestock cannot reach.

Recent research has found that as much as two-thirds of the sparse rainfall in the Sahel consists of water evaporated from plants and the soil, not from the ocean. Overgrazing has removed the plants that provided much of the land's moisture, and *erosion* has reduced the ability of the soil to hold water. As a result there is still less evaporation, and less rainfall. Much of the area thus becomes desert.

Restoring grasslands in places where they have been damaged by overgrazing or over-intensive farming is a major challenge. It would involve persuading the people living in the area to look elsewhere for grazing and food. It is hard to imagine a way of restoring the Sahel, for example, without somehow providing an alternative food supply for many thousands of people.

In countries where the population is not so poor, protecting semi-natural grassland is more feasible. Where farmers have enough land to move their flocks and herds to fresh pastures, leaving other areas to regrow, the grassland will survive indefinitely.

Conservation and Tourism

Alpine pastures in Austria and Switzerland are protected by local governments, because they are recognized as a major tourist asset. Farmers cut hay in much the same way as their grandfathers did, often still using *scythes* (though some use small mechanical mowers), and dry it in huts in the mountain meadows. From there it is carried to the valleys to feed the cattle when they are taken down from the high pastures in winter. No pesticides are used anywhere in the mountains. The result is some of the best-preserved grassland in Europe, full of wildflowers, butterflies and grasshoppers—and a flourishing population of horseflies that feed on the cattle, and on passing walkers.

The great national parks in southern and eastern Africa were originally set up as hunting reserves during the days when the the British Empire ruled this region. With independence, countries like Kenya, Tanzania, Zambia and Zimbabwe recognized that the parks and their wildlife attracted tourists, who brought much-needed money into the country. The newly independent African governments maintained the parks as a source of income. However, they are under pressure today from poaching—the illegal hunting of elephants for their ivory and rhinos for their horns, and also for "bush meat," the meat of wild animals. Defending the parks against poaching requires money for game wardens, which the governments can ill afford. Today, also, with rising populations in these countries, there is a heavy demand for new farming land, and hungry eyes are looking at the national parks. Outside the parks, little of the savannah survives, as we have seen. The national parks

Llamas and alpacas graze in the mountains near Arequipa, Peru. The paramo pastures offer good grazing for livestock in summer.

Tourists admire a lion while on safari in the Serengeti National Park in Tanzania.

of Africa may be safe for the time being, but their survival will depend on continued income from tourism.

Tourism depends in its turn on safe and secure air travel. If people are scared to fly, or few people have the money to do so, the land may one day become more valuable as a place to grow food.

Grasslands and Climate Change

The most serious long-term threat to grasslands may be the change in the global climate, which most scientists believe to be caused by rising levels of carbon dioxide in the atmosphere. The effect of this is not just to make the Earth warmer, but also to alter the patterns of rainfall worldwide. Places that are now too dry to support grasslands may possibly become wetter, but places where grass now grows—including farmland where wheat and other human food crops are cultivated—may become either too wet or too dry. Climate changes such as this have happened in the past—one of them gave rise to grasslands 65 million years ago, in the Cenozoic era. But in the past such changes took place over millions of years, giving plants time to evolve to meet the challenge. The changes in climate over the last 150 years or so have occurred too quickly for the grasslands to adapt.

Grasslands have a problem compared with other biomes: they are not visibly in danger, and they are not as glamorous as rainforests and oceans. Huge wheat fields look healthy: it is easy to overlook the habitat destruction that they represent. In contrast, overgrazed pastures seem beyond salvation: it seems easier to send food to the people whose pastureland has been ruined than to restore their pastures. It is possible to repair the damage done by centuries of

Educational Video

Scan here to watch a short video on grasslands conservation in the U.S.:

misuse or neglect, if only the money can be found. A lot of research has been done, but to apply it needs action not by governments but by the people whose lives depend on the land.

The Effects of Humans

Human domination of the world's grasslands has changed most of them from their original condition. Rolling hills covered in flowers and insects have become orderly crop plantations. At first this happened on a small scale, but when farming became an industry whole landscapes were permanently altered. A number of animal and plant species have disappeared completely, and others are endangered. Present ways of grazing cattle in developed countries are causing serious harm to grasslands: in many developing countries, this damage is beyond repair.

Plowing and heavy overgrazing can both destroy plant life. Plowing destroys the original plant cover completely especially if it is followed by the regular use of weedkillers. The crop plants that replace the natural plant cover may provide homes for some animals—the harvest mouse in Europe, for example, lives comfortably among tall wheat stems. However, crop plants are of no use to most animal species.

Overgrazing causes more subtle changes. While it is true that grass grows better when it is nibbled off, there is a limit to the damage it can survive. As we have seen, many plants have defenses against being eaten. The end result of heavy overgrazing will be that all the edible grasses are gone, leaving behind stands of thistles and docks and other non-edible plants. On the other hand some plants, such as certain species of orchid, are adapted to living on grazed land, so long as it is not over-grazed. These species cannot live anywhere else.

The first enemies of farmers were the predators that threatened their livestock. Since the earliest times, tigers, lions, and wolves have been under attack from farmers. Today, these large predators are rare or endangered. In recent times protections have been put in place, but typically the predators are kept in remote reserves where they pose no threat to farmers or their livestock. In the United States, protected predators include cougars, coyotes, and wolves.

Other animals have come under pressure because they are a nuisance rather than a threat. Prairie dogs undermine cattle ranges, causing accidents when animals fall into the honey-

 ## Saving Endangered Animals

In 1987 the black-footed ferret in Wyoming, a small grasslands predator that lives on prairie dogs, was so close to extinction that the last 18 known survivors were taken in and bred in captivity. Thanks to this breeding program, run by the U.S. Fish and Wildlife Service, black-footed ferrets were re-introduced to wild grasslands in eight western U.S. states and Mexico between 1991 and 2008. Today, although the species is still considered "endangered," there are more than 1,000 black-footed ferrets living in the wild.

combed ground. Consequently, many ranchers poison them to protect their stock. But prairie dogs and their "towns" are an important part of the prairie ecosystem. In Europe, moles have been persecuted as pests in a similar way. Like prairie dogs they undermine the ground, but they can also contaminate silage, causing it to rot rather than produce sweet cattle feed. However, moles are triumphant survivors, even though they have been persecuted for hundreds of years.

Ground-nesting birds are often accidental victims of farming. Crop plants often grow too tall for them to nest among, and pesticides wipe out the insects they feed on. In pastures, cattle trample their nests and eat the grass that the birds require for cover. One badly affected species on the North American prairies is the burrowing owl, which needs undisturbed grassland for nesting, and is vulnerable to trampling by cattle. Birds of prey have suffered too, partly because grazing reduces the cover where their prey lives.

In some parts of the United States and Europe, farmers have begun sowing cereals in winter, rather than in spring. This has had a serious effect on ground-nesting birds such as skylarks. These birds need short plants, or stubble, for nesting, but by the time the skylarks nest, winter-sown cereals are too tall. The few suitable breeding areas are overcrowded, and many birds respond by not breeding at all.

What Can Be Done?

The best chance for saving the grasslands is at the local level. Overgrazing is a major cause of grassland destruction, and it is a local problem. Reducing the number of cattle in an area is not always possible, because in some places cattle are regarded as status symbols and people are not willing to give them up. Finding another source of food for the cattle has helped in some places, where it has been possible to grow trees and shrubs with nutritious leaves for the cattle to eat. Elsewhere, irrigation has helped to water grasslands that had become too dry to support cattle. Although only a few overgrazed pastures have been restored, this approach is better for the environment than abandoning ruined grasslands. It is not only the farmers who benefit, but all the animals and plants with which they share the land.

Text-Dependent Questions

1. What region of Africa has been terribly affected by overgrazing?
2. Why do the Austrian and Swiss governments protect Alpine pastures?
3. What is the most serious long-term threat to grasslands?

Research Project

Using your school library or the internet, do some research to answer the question, "Should farming techniques be changed to protect wildlife?" Some scientists will argue that techniques should be changed, because it is important to maintain the biodiversity of agricultural land, and it is possible to farm land profitably in ways that will protect wildlife. Others contend that intensive farming produces more food per acre, and humans need to produce as much food as possible for their own survival. Write a two-page report, using data and examples to support your conclusion.

Grasslands

Grasslands are lands dominated by grasses, rather than large shrubs or trees. There are two main types of grasslands. These include tropical grasslands and temperate grasslands. Tropical grasslands grow where there is a marked difference between wet and dry seasons. The dry season is usually longer than the wet, and is between two and eleven months long.

Savannah is a type of tropical grassland that grows within 8° and 20° of the Equator. These lands receive between 30 and 60 inches (80 and 150 cm) of rain per year, and rainfall is strongly seasonal. The three types are wet savannah, where the dry season is between three and five months; dry savannah, where the dry season is five to seven months; and thornbush, the driest type, where long droughts are frequent. Savannas cover almost half the surface of Africa (about five million square miles), as well as large areas of Australia, South America, and India.

Temperate grasslands grow where rainfall is between 10 and 30 inches (25 and 75 cm) per year. The rain in these regions falls throughout the year, rather than during one season. Temperate grasslands, also known as steppes, have hot summers and cold winters. They can be found in North

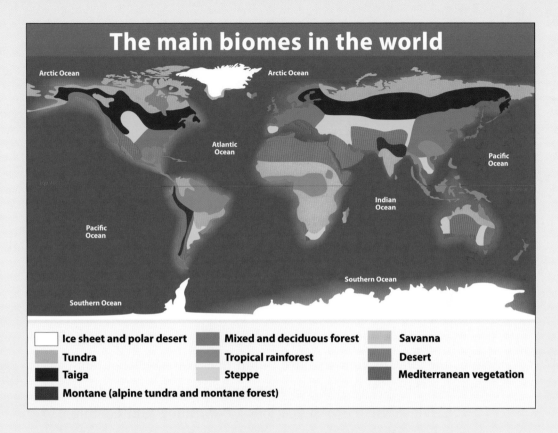

The main biomes in the world

Arctic Ocean   Arctic Ocean

Atlantic Ocean

Pacific Ocean

Equator

Indian Ocean

Pacific Ocean

Southern Ocean

Southern Ocean

Ice sheet and polar desert	Mixed and deciduous forest	Savanna
Tundra	Tropical rainforest	Desert
Taiga	Steppe	Mediterranean vegetation
Montane (alpine tundra and montane forest)		

America, as well as the veldts of South Africa, the puszta of Hungary, the pampas of Argentina and Uruguay, and the steppes of Asia.

Prairies are a type of temperate grassland found in the western part of the United States. Prairies can be divided into three types: short-grass prairies, long-grass prairies, and mixed or mid-grass prairies.

Short-grass prairies grow in the rain shadow of the Rocky Mountains, where the annual rainfall averages 12 inches (30 cm). Their grass cover is made up of drought-tolerant species, growing about 6 to 12 inches (15 to 30 cm) tall. Long-grass prairies occupy about one-third of the central United States, where the rainfall averages about 35 inches (90 cm) per year. In wild areas that are not farmed, grasses can grow to 6-12 feet (2–4 m) tall. The area between the two is known as mid-grass prairie. The grass height varies depending on the local weather and topography.

Appendix

Climate Change

The Earth's climate has changed throughout history. During the last 650,000 years there have been seven cycles of glacial advance and retreat. The end of the last ice age, about 11,700 years ago, marks the beginning of the modern climate era—and of human civilization.

Today, the Earth is experiencing another warming period. Since the 1950s scientists have found that average global temperatures have gradually risen by more than 1° Fahrenheit (0.6° Celsius). In the past, periods of warming and cooling have been attributed to very small variations in Earth's orbit that change the amount of solar energy our planet receives. Two things make the current warming trend unusual. First, most scientists agree that the warming is probably caused by human activities that release carbon dioxide into the atmosphere. Second, the speed at which the Earth's temperature is rising is much faster than this phenomenon has ever occurred in the past, according to climate records.

The heat-trapping nature of carbon dioxide and other "greenhouse gases" was demonstrated in the mid-19th century. Without the Earth's atmosphere, the sun's energy would be reflected back into space. Greenhouse gases in the atmosphere trap some of the sun's heat, reflecting it back to keep the earth's

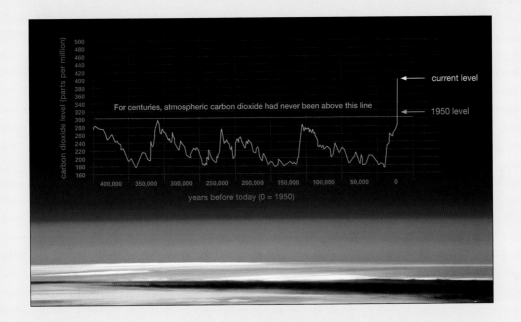

Chart showing carbon dioxide level (parts per million) versus years before today (0 = 1950). Y-axis ranges from 160 to 500. X-axis shows 400,000; 350,000; 300,000; 250,000; 200,000; 150,000; 100,000; 50,000; 0. Label at the 300 line: "For centuries, atmospheric carbon dioxide had never been above this line". Arrows point to "current level" and "1950 level".

surface warmer than it would otherwise be. Without the atmosphere, the Earth's average temperature would be 0°F (–18°C). Thanks to the greenhouse effect, Earth's average temperature is currently about 59°F (15°C).

Increased levels of greenhouse gases in the atmosphere must cause the Earth to warm in response. Since the start of the Industrial Revolution in the mid-eighteenth century, human activities—including the burning of "fossil fuels" like oil, coal, and natural gas, as well as farming and the clearing of large forested areas—have produced a 40 percent increase in the atmospheric concentration of carbon dioxide, from 280 parts per million (ppm) in 1750 to over 400 ppm today.

Scientists understand how the Earth's climate has changed over the past 650,000 years by studying ice cores drawn from Greenland, Antarctica, and tropical mountain glaciers. Varying

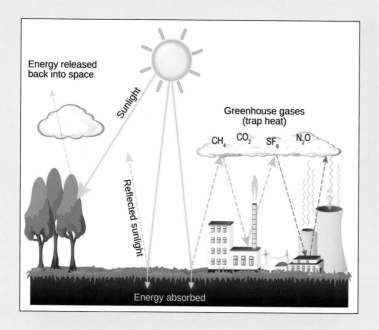

carbon dioxide levels found in the ancient ice show how the Earth's climate responds to changes in greenhouse gas levels. Ancient evidence can also be found in tree rings, ocean sediments, coral reefs, and layers of sedimentary rocks. This ancient, or paleoclimate, evidence reveals that current warming is occurring roughly ten times faster than the average rate of ice-age-recovery warming.

Most scientists believe that if greenhouse gas emissions continue at the present rate, Earth's surface temperature could grow much warmer than it has been in more than 650,000 years. Recent studies indicate that, if emissions are not reduced, the Earth could warm by another 3.6°F (2°C) over the next twenty years. This would have an extremely harmful effect on ecosystems, biodiversity, and the livelihoods of people worldwide.

Evidence of Climate Change

Earth's average surface temperature has risen about 2°F (1.1°C) since the late nineteenth century. Most of this warming has occurred over the past 35 years. Seventeen of the eighteen warmest years in recorded history have occurred since 2001, and 2017 was the warmest year on record.

Oceans have absorbed much of the increased heat, with the top 2,300 feet (700 meters) of ocean warming by 0.3°F since 1969.

The Greenland and Antarctic ice sheets have melted greatly over the past thirty years. Further melting of the ice sheets could result in significant rise in sea levels.

The strength and frequency of hurricanes and other extreme storms has risen along with global temperatures.

Series Glossary

atmosphere—an envelope of gases that surrounds the earth (or another planet). Earth's atmosphere, which is composed of mostly nitrogen and oxygen, helps the earth retain heat and reflect ultraviolet radiation.

biodiversity—the variety among and within plant and animal species in a particular environment.

biomass—the total of all living organisms in a given area.

biome—a very large ecological area, with plants and animals that are adapted to the environmental conditions there. Biomes are usually defined by their physical characteristics—such as climate, geology, or vegetation—rather than by the animals that live there.

climate—the long-term average weather pattern in a particular place.

climate change—a change in global or regional climate patterns. This term is generally used to refer to changes that have become apparent since the mid- to late-twentieth century that are attributed in large part to the increased levels of atmospheric carbon dioxide produced by the use of fossil fuels.

ecology—the scientific study of animals and plants in their natural surroundings.

ecosystem—all the living things, from plants and animals to microscopic organisms, that share and interact within a particular area.

food chain—a group of organisms interrelated by the fact that each member of the group feeds upon the one below it.

genus—a group of closely related species.

geodiversity—the variety of earth materials (such as minerals, rocks, or sediments) and processes (such as erosion or volcanic activity) that constitute and shape the Earth.

global warming—a gradual increase in the overall temperature of the earth's atmosphere. It is generally attributed to the greenhouse effect, caused by increased levels of carbon dioxide, chlorofluorocarbons, and other pollutants in the atmosphere.

greenhouse effect—a term used to describe warming of the atmosphere owing to the presence of carbon dioxide and other gases. Without the presence of these gases, heat from the sun would return to space in the form of infrared radiation. Carbon dioxide and other gases absorb some of this radiation and prevent its release, thereby warming the earth.

habitat—the natural home of a particular plant or animal species.

invasive species—a non-native species that, when introduced to an area, is likely to cause economic or environmental damage or harm to human health.

nutrient—chemical elements and compounds that provide organisms with the necessary nourishment.

species—a group of similar animals or plants that can breed together naturally and produce normal offspring.

umbrella species—a species selected for making conservation-related decisions, because protecting these species indirectly protects many other species that make up the ecological community of its habitat.

vegetation—ground cover provided by plants.

watershed—the land where water from rain and melted snow drains downhill into a body of water, such as a river, lake, reservoir, estuary, wetland, sea, or ocean.

Further Reading

Bow, James. *Grasslands Inside Out*. New York: Crabtree Publishing, 2015.

Dawson, Ashley. *Extinction: A Radical History*. London: OR Books, 2016.

Johansson, Philip. *The Grasslands: Discover this Wide-Open Biome*. Berkeley Heights, N.J.: Enslow, 2015.

Joppa, Lucas N., Jonathan E.M. Bailie, and John G. Robinson, eds. *Protected Areas: Are They Safeguarding Biodiversity?* Hoboken, N.J.: John Wiley and Sons, Ltd., 2016.

Kareiva, Peter, and Michelle Marvier. *Conservation Science: Balancing the Needs of People and Nature*. 2nd ed. New York: W.H. Freeman, 2014.

Kolbert, Elizabeth. *The Sixth Extinction: An Unnatural History*. New York: Henry Holt and Co., 2014.

Rice, William B. *African Grasslands*. Huntington Beach, Calif.: Teacher Created Materials, 2012.

Taylor, Dorceta E. *The Rise of the American Conservation Movement: Power, Privilege, and Environmental Protection*. Durham, N.C.: Duke University Press, 2016.

Internet Resources

www.worldwildlife.org
The World Wildlife Fund (WWF) was founded in 1961 as an international fundraising organization, which works in collaboration with conservation groups to protect animals and their natural habitats.

www.audubon.org
The National Audubon Society is one of the oldest conservation organizations. It uses science, education, and grassroots advocacy to protect birds and their habitats around the world.

www.iucn.org
The International Union for Conservation of Nature (IUCN) includes both government and non-governmental organizations. It works to provide knowledge and tools so that economic development and nature conservation can take place together.

http://www.nwf.org
The National Wildlife Federation is the largest grassroots conservation organization in the United States, with over 6 million supporters and affiliated organizations in every state.

Publisher's Note: The websites listed on this page were active at the time of publication. The publisher is not responsible for websites that have changed their address or discontinued operation since the date of publication. The publisher reviews and updates the websites each time the book is reprinted.

www.fws.gov

The U.S. Fish and Wildlife Service is a branch of the government that is responsible for enforcing federal wildlife laws, protecting endangered species, and conserving and restoring wildlife habitats within the United States.

www.nmfs.noaa.gov

NOAA Fisheries is responsible for the stewardship of the nation's ocean resources, including the recovery and conservation of protected water habitats to promote healthy ecosystems.

www.nature.org

The Nature Conservancy is a leading conservation organization. It works in more than 70 countries to protect ecologically important lands and waters all over the world.

www.sierraclub.org

Founded by legendary conservationist John Muir in 1892, the Sierra Club is among the largest and most influential environmental organizations in the United States. The organization has protected millions of acres of wilderness, and helped to pass the Clean Air Act, Clean Water Act, and Endangered Species Act.

http://www.greenpeace.org

Greenpeace uses protests and creative communication to expose global environmental problems and promote solutions that are essential to a green and peaceful future.

Index

Numbers in **bold italic** refer to captions.

farming, *20*, 46, 47, *48, 54, 55*, 57, 58, 59, 62, *65*, 69
Fertile Crescent, 46
fire, 8, *9*, 13, 14, 19, *20*, 22, 23, 25, 31
flies, 39
food chain, *11*, 33, 37
foxes, 37
foxglove, *21*

gauchos, 16
gazelles, *33*
giraffes, 15, 34
goats, 34, *35*, 46, 49, 51, *52*
gophers, 37
grain crops, 25
grasshoppers, 38, 43, 58

habitat destruction, 61
hamburgers, 58
harvest mouse, 62
hawks, 37
hay, 25, 58
herbicides, 48
horses, *16*, *19*, 33, 34, *36*, 51, *53*
hunter-gatherers, 45, 46, 48

India, *49*
insects, 12, 27, 38, 39, *40*, 48, 62, 64
irrigation, 31, 46, 65

jackals, 33, 37

kangaroo, *26*
Kansas, *7*

lions, 12, 33, 36, 43
locusts, 39

Madagascar, *20, 50*
maize, 16, 46, 48
mammals, 17, *35*, 37, 39, 43
marmots, 37
Masai Mara Reserve, Kenya, *33*
Maxwell Wildlife Refuge, Kansas, *7*
mice, 12, 33
Middle East, 46, 52
moles, 36, 64

Mongolia, *19*, 28, 51, *53*
mongooses, 37
Montana, *36*

national parks, 58, 59
Native American people, 8, 27, 31, 47, 48
nematodes, 11, *17*
New Zealand, 17, 28
nomadic people, 51
North America, 7, 8, 12, 14, 30, *37, 43*, 47, 66, 67
nutrients, 8

oats, 48, 55
ostriches, 41, 42
outback, 8, 26
overgrazing, 51, *52, 55*, 57, 58, 62, 64, *65*

pampa, 7, 16, 31, 67
paramo, 15, 28, *59*
Patagonia, *16*
Peru, *59*
pesticides, 48, 64
pioneer plants, 20, 21
plant succession, 19, 25
plowing, *30*, 31, 48, 62
poisonous plants, 24
poppy, *24*
prairie dogs, *37*, 43, 63, 64
prairies, 7, 8, 12, 13, 14, *30*, 31, *37*, 64, 67
primates, 33
pulses, 54
pumas, 33

quelea, 41

rabbits, 37
rainfall, 8, 13, 57, 58, 61, 66, 67
reserves, 58, 63
rheas, 41, 42
rhinoceros, 34
rice, 46, *47*, 48, 54, *55*
rodents, 33, 37
rumination, 34, 35, *43*

Sahel, 7, 28, 57, 58

savannah, 8, 12, 13, 14, *15*, 28, 33, 41, 43, 59, 66
secretary bird, 43
semi-natural grasslands, 8, 28, 57, 58
Serengeti National Park, Tanzania, *60*
sheep, *16*, 17, *26*, *27*, 34, *35*, 36, 46, 49, 51
shrubs, 8, 21, 22, *52*, 65, 66
silage, 25, 64
silicon, 34
slash and burn cultivation, *20*
soil, 8, 9, *10*, 11, 12, 25, 26, *27*, 36, 48, 57, 58
sorghum, 48, *49, 55*
South Africa, *39, 42*, 67
South America, 15, 16, 66
steppes, 7, 28, 66, 67
stoats, 12
Switzerland, *56*, 58

Tanzania, *60*
tapirs, 34
teeth, 34
temperate climate, 21
temperate grasslands, 7, 14, 22, 66
terraces, 46, *47*
thistles, 22, 23, 29, 62

tigers, 63
tourism, 28, 58, 60
trees, 7, 8, *14*, 15, *20*, 21, 22, 31, 41, 52, 65, 66
tropical grasslands, 7, 15, 22, 66
tussock grassland, 17

United States, *37*, 43, *45, 49*, 50, 63, 64, 67
U.S. Fish and Wildlife Service, *63*

voles, 12
vultures, 43

wallabie, *26*
weasels, 12
weedkillers, 62
weeds, 20, *24*, 25, 46, 48
wheat, 16, *30*, 43, *45*, 48, 54, *55*, 61, 62
wild grasslands, 13, 28, *29, 37*
wildebeest, 8, 11, 12
wildflowers, 38, 58
wolves, 12, 63
Wyoming, 63

yurts, 51, 53

About the Author

Kimberly Sidabras is a freelance writer and editor. She worked with the World Wildlife Federation for nearly two decades. A graduate of Temple University, she lives near Philadelphia with her husband and three children. She is the author of five volumes in the WORLD'S BIOMES series (Mason Crest, 2019).

Picture Credits: National Aeronautics and Space Administration: 69; © OTTN Publishing: 67, 70; used under license from Shutterstock, Inc.: 1, 2, 9, 11, 14, 15, 16, 18, 20, 21, 23, 24, 26, 29, 30, 32, 35, 36, 38, 39, 40, 42, 44, 47, 49, 50, 52, 53, 54, 57, 59, 71; Chantal de Bruijne / Shutterstock.com: 60; Michael Rosebrock / Shutterstock.com: 6.